Healthy Air Fryer Cookbook

Learn How to Fry, Bake, Grill and Roast Delicious and Low-Fat Recipes with Your Air Fryer

Linda Wang

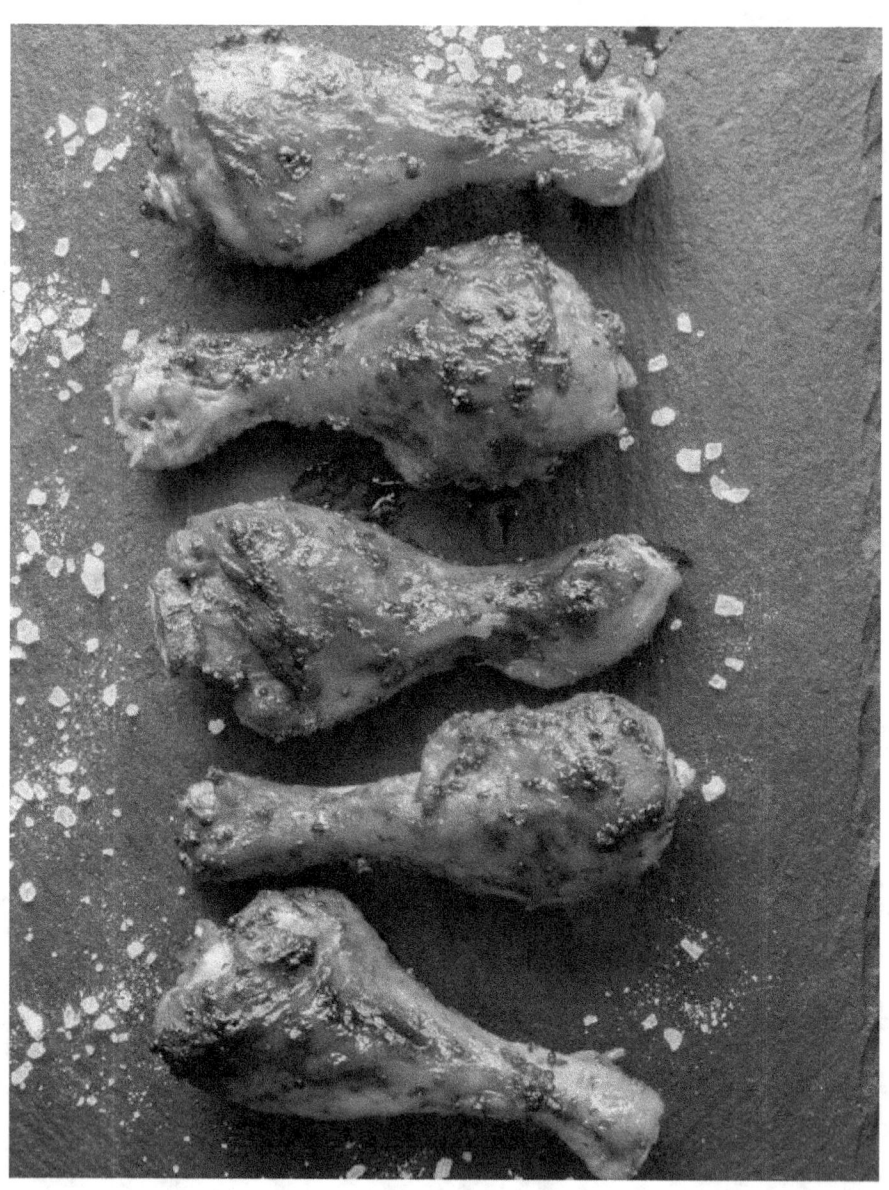

© **Copyright 2021 by Linda Wang - All rights reserved.**

The content contained within this book may not be reproduced, duplicated or transmitted without direct written permission from the author or the publisher.
Under no circumstances will any blame or legal responsibility be held against the publisher, or author, for any damages, reparation, or monetary loss due to the information contained within this book. Either directly or indirectly.

Legal Notice:
This book is copyright protected. This book is only for personal use. You cannot amend, distribute, sell, use, quote or paraphrase any part, or the content within this book, without the consent of the author or publisher.

Disclaimer Notice:
Please note the information contained within this document is for educational and entertainment purposes only. All effort has been executed to present accurate, up to date, and reliable, complete information. No warranties of any kind are declared or implied. Readers acknowledge that the author is not engaging in the rendering of legal, financial, medical or professional advice. The content within this book has been derived from various sources. Please consult a licensed professional before attempting any techniques outlined in this book.
By reading this document, the reader agrees that under no circumstances is the author responsible for any losses, direct or indirect, which are incurred as a result of the use of information contained within this document, including, but not limited to, — errors, omissions, or inaccuracies.

TABLE OF CONTENTS

INTRODUCTION 1

Vegetable Quiche 5

Strawberries Oatmeal 7

Stuffed Poblanos 9

Coriander Potatoes 11

Sweet Potato and Eggplant Mix 13

Healthy Kidney Beans Oatmeal 15

Tilapia Fish Fillets 17

Buttered Scallops 19

Buttered Crab Shells 21

Rice in Crab Shell 23

Trout and Zucchinis 25

Shrimp and Tomatoes 27

Trout Bites 28

Chicken with Veggies and Rice 29

Herbed Duck Legs 31

Chicken Wings with Prawn Paste 33

Chicken Breasts with Chimichurri 35

Asian Atyle Chicken 37

Crispy Honey Chicken Wings 39

Garlic Chicken Nuggets 41

Lamb and Macadamia Nuts Mix 43

Beef, Cucumber and Eggplants 44

Spicy Lamb Kebabs 46

Pepper Pork Chops 49

Pork Chops with Chicory Treviso 51

Beef and Celery 53

Beef Kabobs Recipe 54

Sautéed Green Beans 56

Simple Kale Chicken Soup 58

Healthy Chicken Vegetable Soup 60

Chicken Rice Noodle Soup 62

Asparagus Garlic Ham Soup 64

Air fryer Greek Beef Stew 66

Mushroom Chicken Soup 68

Classic ratatouille (Vegan) 70

Curried Eggplant (Vegan) 72

Stuffed Tomatoes (Vegan) 74

Sweet and Spicy Grilled Chicken 76

Honey Lime Grilled Chicken 78

Pesto Grilled Chicken 80

Easy Curry Grilled Chicken Wings 81

PiriPiri Chicken 83

Air Fryer Plantains 84

Healthy Veggie Lasagna 86

Dark Chocolate Cheesecake 88

Lemon Coconut Pie 90

Pumpkin Cake 92

Easy Baked Chocolate Mug Cake 94

Crisped 'n Chewy Chonut Holes 96

Cream Puffs 98

NOTES 101

INTRODUCTION

An Air Fryer is a magic revolutionized kitchen appliance that helps you fry with less or even no oil at all. This kind of product applies Rapid Air technology, which offers a new way to fry with less oil. This new invention cooks food through the circulation of superheated air and generates 80% low-fat food. Although the food is fried with less oil, you don't need to worry as the food processed by the Air Fryer still has the same taste like the food fried using the deep-frying method.

This technology uses a superheated element, which radiates heat close to the food and an exhaust fan in its lid to circulate airflow. An Air Fryer ensures that the food processed is cooked completely. The exhaust fan located at the top of the cooking chamber helps the food get the same heating temperature in every part quickly, resulting in a cooked food of better and healthier quality. Besides, cooking with an Air Fryer is also suitable for those individuals which are too busy or do not have enough time. For example, an Air Fryer only needs half a spoonful of oil and takes 10 minutes to serve a medium bowl of crispy French fries.

In addition to serving healthier food, an Air Fryer also provides some other benefits to you. Since an Air Fryer helps you fry using less oil or without oil for some kind of food, it automatically reduces the fat and cholesterol content in food. Indeed, no one will refuse to enjoy fried food without worrying about the greasy and fat content. Having fried food with no guilt is one of the pleasures of life. Besides having low fat and cholesterol, you save some amount of money by consuming oil sparingly, which can be used for other needs. An Air Fryer also can reheat your food. Sometimes, when you have fried leftover and you reheat it, it will usually serve reheated greasy food with some addition of unhealthy reuse oil. Undoubtedly, the saturated fat in the fried food gets worse because of this process. An Air Fryer helps you reheat your food without being afraid of extra oils that the food may absorb. Fried bananas, fish and chips, nuggets, or even fried chicken can be reheated to become as warm and crispy as they were before by using an Air Fryer.

Some people may think that spending some amount of money to buy a fryer is wasteful. I dare to say that they are wrong because an Air Fryer is not only used to fry. It is a sophisticated multi-function appliance since it also helps you to roast chicken, make steak, grill fish, and even bake a cake. With a built-in air filter, an Air Fryer filters the air and saves your kitchen from smoke and grease.

An air Fryer is really a new innovative method of cooking. Grab it fast and welcome to a clean and healthy kitchen.

Vegetable Quiche

Preparation Time: 10 minutes

Cooking Time: 24 minutes

Serve: 6

Ingredients:

- 8 eggs
- 1 cup tomatoes, chopped
- 1 onion, chopped
- 1 cup coconut milk
- 1 cup zucchini, chopped
- 1 tbsp butter
- 1 cup Parmesan cheese, grated
- 1/2 tsp pepper
- 1 tsp salt

Directions:

1. Preheat the air fryer to 370 °F.
2. Melt butter in a pan over medium heat then add onion and sauté until onion lightly brown.

3. Add tomatoes and zucchini to the pan and sauté for 4-5 minutes.
4. Transfer cooked vegetables into the air fryer baking dish.
5. Beat eggs with cheese, milk, pepper, and salt in a bowl.
6. Pour egg mixture over vegetables in a baking dish.
7. Place the dish in the air fryer and cook for 24 minutes or until eggs are set.
8. Slice and serve.

Nutrition:

Calories 255, Fat 16 g, Carbohydrates 8 g, Sugar 4.2 g, Protein 21 g, Cholesterol 257 mg

Strawberries Oatmeal

Preparation Time: 20 minutes

Servings: 4

Ingredients:

- ¼ cup strawberries
- ½ cup coconut; shredded
- 2 cups coconut milk
- ¼ tsp. vanilla extract

- 2 tsp. stevia
- Cooking spray

Directions:

1. Grease the Air Fryer's pan with the cooking spray, add all the ingredients inside and toss
2. Cook at 365 °F for 15 minutes, divide into bowls and serve for breakfast

Nutrition:

Calories: 142; Fat: 7g; Fiber: 2g; Carbs: 3g; Protein: 5g

Stuffed Poblanos

Preparation Time: 30 minutes

Servings: 4

Ingredients:

- 4 large eggs.
- ½ lb. spicy ground pork breakfast sausage
- 8 tbsp. shredded pepper jack cheese
- 4 large poblano peppers
- ½ cup full-fat sour cream.
- 4 oz. full-fat cream cheese; softened.
- ¼ cup canned diced tomatoes and green chiles, drained

Directions:

1. In a medium skillet over medium heat, crumble and brown the ground sausage until no pink remains. Remove sausage and drain the fat from the pan. Crack eggs into the pan, scramble and cook until no longer runny

2. Place cooked sausage in a large bowl and fold in cream cheese. Mix in diced tomatoes and chiles. Gently fold in eggs
3. Cut a 4"-5" slit in the top of each poblano, removing the seeds and white membrane with a small knife. Separate the filling into four and spoon carefully into each pepper. Top each with 2 tbsp. pepper jack cheese
4. Place each pepper into the air fryer basket. Adjust the temperature to 350 Degrees F and set the timer for 15 minutes.
5. Peppers will be soft and cheese will be browned when ready. Serve immediately with sour cream on top.

Nutrition:

Calories: 489; Protein: 22.8g; Fiber: 3.8g; Fat: 35.6g; Carbs: 12.6g

Coriander Potatoes

Preparation Time: 10 minutes

Cooking time: 25 minutes

Servings: 4

Ingredients:

- 1 pound gold potatoes, peeled and cut into wedges

- 1 tablespoon tomato sauce
- 2 tablespoons coriander, chopped
- ½ teaspoon garlic powder
- 1 teaspoon chili powder
- Salt and black pepper to the taste
- 1 tablespoon olive oil

Directions:

1. In a bowl, combine the potatoes with the tomato sauce and the other ingredients, toss, and transfer to the air fryer's basket.
2. Cook at 370 degrees F for 25 minutes, divide between plates and serve as a side dish.

Nutrition:

Calories 210, fat 5, fiber 7, carbs 12, protein 5

Sweet Potato and Eggplant Mix

Preparation Time: 10 minutes

Cooking time: 20 minutes

Servings: 4

Ingredients:
- 2 eggplants, roughly cubed
- 2 sweet potatoes, peeled and cut into medium wedges

- 4 garlic cloves, minced
- 1 tablespoon avocado oil
- Juice of 1 lemon
- 1 teaspoon nutmeg, ground
- Salt and black pepper to the taste
- 1 tablespoon rosemary, chopped

Directions:

1. In your air fryer, combine the potatoes with the eggplants and the other Ingredients, toss and cook at 370 degrees F for 20 minutes.
2. Divide the mix between plates and serve as a side dish.

Nutrition:

Calories 182, fat 6, fiber 3, carbs 11, protein 5

Healthy Kidney Beans Oatmeal

Preparation Time: 25 minutes

Servings: 2 – 4

Ingredients:

- 2 large bell peppers; halved lengthwise, deseeded
- 2 tablespoon cooked chick peas
- 2 tablespoon cooked kidney beans
- 1/4 cup yogurt
- 2 cups oatmeal; cooked
- 1 teaspoon ground cumin
- 1/2 teaspoon paprika
- 1/2 teaspoon salt or to taste
- 1/4 teaspoon black pepper powder

Directions:

1. Place the bell peppers with its cut side down in the Air Fryer. Air fry in a preheated Air Fryer at 355 - degrees Fahrenheit for 2 – 3 minutes.

2. Remove from the Air Fryer and keep it aside.
3. Mix together the rest of the ingredients in a bowl.
4. When the bell peppers are cool enough to handle, divide and stuff this mixture into the bell peppers.
5. Place it back in the Air Fryer and air fry at 355 – degrees Fahrenheit for 4 minutes. Serve hot and enjoy!.

Tilapia Fish Fillets

Preparation Time: 10 minutes

Cooking Time: 7 minutes

Serve: 2

Ingredients:

- 2 tilapia fillets
- 1/2 tsp butter
- 1 tsp old bay seasoning
- 1/4 tsp lemon pepper

- Pepper
- Salt

Directions:

1. Spray air fryer basket with cooking spray.
2. Place fish fillets into the air fryer basket and season with lemon pepper, old bay seasoning, pepper, and salt.
3. Spray fish fillets with cooking spray and cook at 400 °F for 7 minutes.
4. Serve and enjoy.

Nutrition:

Calories 80, Fat 2 g, Carbohydrates 0.2 g, Sugar 0 g, Protein 15 g, Cholesterol 45 mg

Buttered Scallops

Preparation Time: 15 minutes

Cooking Time: 4 minutes

Servings: 2

Ingredients:

- ¾ pound sea scallops, cleaned and patted very dry
- ½ tablespoon fresh thyme, minced
- 1 tablespoon butter, melted
- Salt and black pepper, as required

Directions:

1. Preheat the Air fryer to 390 degrees F and grease an Air fryer basket.
2. Mix scallops, butter, thyme, salt and black pepper in a bowl.
3. Arrange scallops in the Air fryer basket and cook for about 4 minutes.
4. Dish out the scallops in a platter and serve hot.

Nutrition:

Calories: 202, Fat: 7.1g, Carbohydrates: 4.4g, Sugar: 0g, Protein: 28.7g, Sodium: 393mg

Buttered Crab Shells

Preparation Time: 20 minutes

Cooking Time: 10 minutes

Servings: 4

Ingredients:

- 3 eggs
- 4 soft crab shells, cleaned
- 1 cup buttermilk
- 2 cups panko breadcrumb
- 2 tablespoons butter, melted
- 2 teaspoons seafood seasonings
- 1½ teaspoons lemon zest, grated

Directions:

1. Preheat the Air fryer to 375 degrees F and grease an Air fryer basket.
2. Place the buttermilk in a shallow bowl and whisk the eggs in a second bowl.
3. Mix the breadcrumbs, seafood seasoning, and lemon zest in a third bowl.

4. Soak the crab shells into the buttermilk for about 10 minutes, then dip in the eggs.
5. Dredge in the breadcrumb mixture and arrange the crab shells into the Air fryer basket.
6. Cook for about 10 minutes and dish out in a platter.
7. Drizzle melted butter over the crab shells and immediately serve.

Nutrition:

Calories: 521, Fat: 16.8g, Carbohydrates: 11.5g, Sugar: 3.3g, Protein: 47.8g, Sodium: 1100mg

(Note: Seafood Seasoning - Mix the salt, celery seed, dry mustard powder, red pepper, black pepper, bay leaves, paprika, cloves, allspice, ginger, cardamom, and cinnamon together in a bowl until thoroughly combined. Or, you can buy at your local store or on Amazon.

Rice in Crab Shell

Preparation Time: 20 minutes

Cooking Time: 8 minutes

Servings: 2

Ingredients:

- 4 tablespoons crab meat
- 1 bowl cooked rice
- 2 tablespoons butter
- 2 tablespoons Parmesan cheese, shredded
- 2 crab shells
- Paprika, to taste

Directions:

1. Preheat the Air fryer to 390 degrees F and grease an Air fryer basket.
2. Mix rice, crab meat, butter and paprika in a bowl.
3. Fill crab shell with rice mixture and top with Parmesan cheese.

4. Arrange the crab shell in the Air fryer basket and cook for about 8 minutes.
5. Sprinkle with more paprika and serve hot.

Nutrition:

Calories: 285, Fat: 33g, Carbohydrates: 0g, Sugar: 0g, Protein: 33g, Sodium: 153mg

Trout and Zucchinis

Preparation Time: 20 minutes

Servings: 4

Ingredients:

- 3 zucchinis, cut in medium chunks
- ¼ cup tomato sauce
- 4 trout fillets; boneless

- ½ cup cilantro; chopped.
- 1 garlic clove; minced
- 1 tbsp. lemon juice
- 2 tbsp. olive oil
- Salt and black pepper to taste.

Directions:

1. In a pan that fits your air fryer, mix the fish with the other ingredients, toss, introduce in the fryer and cook at 380 °F for 15 minutes. Divide everything between plates and serve right away

Nutrition:

Calories: 220; Fat: 12g; Fiber: 4g; Carbs: 6g; Protein: 9g

Shrimp and Tomatoes

Preparation Time: 25 minutes

Servings: 4

Ingredients:
- 4 onions; chopped.
- 2 lbs. shrimp; peeled and deveined
- 1 lb. tomatoes; peeled and chopped
- 1 tsp. coriander; ground
- 1/4 cup veggie stock
- Juice of 1 lemon
- 4 tbsp. olive oil
- Salt and black pepper to taste

Directions:
1. In a pan that fits your air fryer, mix all the ingredients well
2. Place the pan in the fryer and cook at 360 °F for 15 minutes. Divide into bowls and serve; enjoy!

Trout Bites

Preparation Time: 18 minutes

Servings: 4

Ingredients:

- 1 lb. trout fillets; boneless and cut into cubes
- 1 sweet onion; chopped.
- 1 shallot; sliced
- 2 celery stalks; sliced
- 1 garlic clove; crushed
- 1/3 cup sake
- 1/4 cup miso
- 1/3 cup mirin
- 1-inch ginger piece; chopped
- 1 tsp. mustard
- 1 tsp. sugar
- 1 tbsp. rice vinegar

Directions:

1. Add all ingredients to a pan that fits your air fryer and toss
2. Place the pan in the fryer and cook at 370 °F for 12 minutes. Divide into bowls and serve.

Chicken with Veggies and Rice

Preparation Time: 15 minutes

Cooking Time: 20 minutes

Servings: 3

Ingredients:

- 3 cups cold boiled white rice
- 1 cup cooked chicken, diced
- ½ cup frozen peas
- ½ cup frozen carrots
- ½ cup onion, chopped
- 6 tablespoons soy sauce
- 1 tablespoon vegetable oil

Directions:

1. Preheat the Air fryer to 360 degree F and grease a 7" nonstick pan.
2. Mix the rice, soy sauce, and vegetable oil in a bowl.

3. Stir in the remaining ingredients and mix until well combined.
4. Transfer the rice mixture into the pan and place in the Air fryer.
5. Cook for about 20 minutes and dish out to serve immediately.

Nutrition:

Calories: 405, Fat: 6.4g, Carbohydrates: 63g, Sugar: 3.5g, Protein: 21.7g, Sodium: 1500mg

Herbed Duck Legs

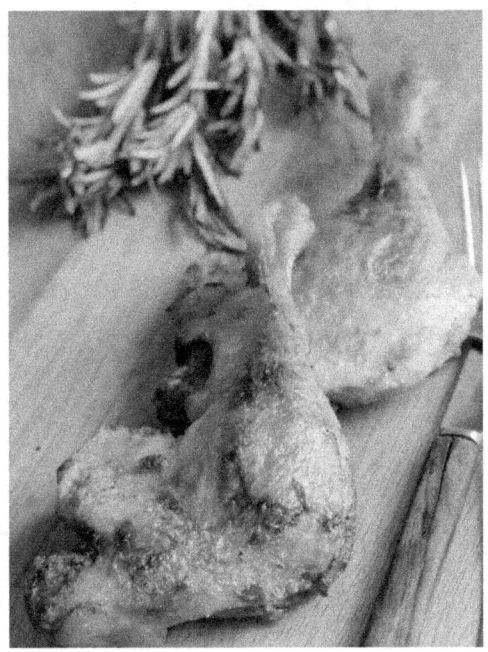

Preparation Time: 10 minutes

Cooking Time: 30 minutes

Servings: 2

Ingredients:

- 2 duck legs
- ½ tablespoon fresh thyme, chopped

- ½ tablespoon fresh parsley, chopped
- 1 garlic clove, minced
- 1 teaspoon five spice powder
- Salt and black pepper, as required

Directions:

1. Preheat the Air fryer to 340 degrees F and grease an Air fryer basket.
2. Mix the garlic, herbs, five-spice powder, salt, and black pepper in a bowl.
3. Rub the duck legs with garlic mixture generously and arrange them into the Air fryer basket.
4. Cook for about 25 minutes and set the Air fryer to 390 degrees F.
5. Cook for 5 more minutes and dish out to serve hot.

Nutrition:

Calories: 138, Fat: 4.5g, Carbohydrates: 1g, Sugar: 0g, Protein: 25g, Sodium: 82mg

Chicken Wings with Prawn Paste

Preparation Time: 20 minutes

Cooking Time: 8 minutes

Servings: 6

Ingredients:

- Corn flour, as required
- 2 pounds mid-joint chicken wings
- 2 tablespoons prawn paste
- 1½ teaspoons sugar
- 4 tablespoons olive oil
- 2 teaspoons sesame oil
- 1 teaspoon Shaoxing wine
- 2 teaspoons fresh ginger juice

Directions:

1. Preheat the Air fryer to 360 degrees F and grease an Air fryer basket.
2. Mix all the ingredients in a bowl except wings and corn flour.

3. Rub the chicken wings generously with marinade and refrigerate overnight.
4. Coat the chicken wings evenly with corn flour and keep aside.
5. Set the Air fryer to 390 degrees F and arrange the chicken wings in the Air fryer basket.
6. Cook for about 8 minutes and dish out to serve hot.

Nutrition:

Calories: 416, Fat: 31.5g, Carbohydrates: 11.2g, Sugar: 1.6g, Protein: 24.4g, Sodium: 661mg

Chicken Breasts with Chimichurri

Preparation Time: 15 minutes

Cooking Time: 35 minutes

Servings: 1

Ingredients:

- Chimichurri
- 1 chicken breast, bone-in, skin-on
- ½ bunch fresh cilantro
- ½ shallot, peeled, cut in quarters
- 1/4 bunch fresh parsley
- ½ tablespoon paprika ground
- ½ tablespoon chili powder
- ½ tablespoon fennel ground
- ½ teaspoon black pepper, ground
- 1 teaspoon salt
- ½ teaspoon onion powder
- ½ teaspoon garlic powder
- ½ teaspoon cumin ground
- ½ tablespoon canola oil

- 2 tablespoons olive oil
- 4 garlic cloves, peeled
- Zest and juice of 1 lemon
- 1 teaspoon kosher salt

Directions:

1. Preheat the Air fryer to 300 degrees F and grease an Air fryer basket.
2. Combine all the spices in a suitable bowl and season the chicken with it.
3. Sprinkle with canola oil and arrange the chicken in the Air fryer basket.
4. Cook for about 35 minutes and dish out in a platter.
5. Put all the ingredients in the blender and blend until smooth.
6. Serve the chicken with chimichurri sauce.

Nutrition:

Calories: 140, Fats: 7.9g, Carbohydrates: 1.8g, Sugar: 7.1g, Proteins: 7.2g, Sodium: 581mg

Asian Atyle Chicken

Preparation Time: 40 minutes

Servings: 4

Ingredients:

- 1½ lbs. chicken drumsticks
- 1 lb. spinach; chopped.
- 15 oz. canned tomatoes; crushed
- 1/4 cup lemon juice
- 1/2 cup chicken stock
- 1/2 cup heavy cream
- 4 garlic cloves; minced
- 1/2 cup cilantro; chopped.
- 1 yellow onion; chopped.
- 2 tbsp. butter; melted
- 1 tbsp. ginger; grated
- 1½ tsp. coriander; ground
- 1½ tsp. paprika
- 1 tsp. turmeric powder
- Salt and black pepper to taste

Directions:

1. Place the butter in a pan that fits your air fryer and heat over medium heat.
2. Add the onions and the garlic, stir and cook for 3 minutes
3. Add the ginger, paprika, coriander, turmeric, salt, pepper and the chicken; toss and cook for 4 minutes more.
4. Add the tomatoes and the stock and stir
5. Place the pan in the fryer and cook at 370 °F for 15 minutes
6. Add the spinach, lemon juice, cilantro and the cream; stir and cook for 5-6 minutes more. Divide everything into bowls and serve.

Crispy Honey Chicken Wings

Cooking Time: 35 minutes

Servings: 8

Ingredients:

- 16 pieces chicken wings
- 3/4 cup potato starch
- 1/4 cup clover honey
- 1/8 cup water; or as needed
- 1/4 cup butter
- 4 tbsp. garlic; minced
- 1/2 tsp. kosher salt

Directions:

1. Rinse and dry the chicken wings. Place potato starch in a bowl and coat chicken wings. Add wings to the air fryer, then cook at 380 °F for 25 minutes, shaking the basket every five minutes
2. Once done, cook again at 400°F for 5-10 minutes. All skin on all wings should be very dry and crisp.

3. Heat a small stainless-steel saucepan on low heat. Melt the butter, then add garlic. Sauté the for 5 minutes. Afterwards, add honey and salt

4. Simmer on low for about 20 minutes, stirring every few minutes so the sauce does not burn. Add a few drops of water after 15 minutes to keep sauce from hardening.

5. Remove chicken wings from air fryer and pour sauce over. Coat and serve.

Garlic Chicken Nuggets

Cooking Time: 10 minutes

Servings: 4

Ingredients:

- 9 oz. chicken breast; thinly chopped
- 2 eggs; divided
- 3/4 cup breadcrumbs
- 1 tsp. tomato ketchup

- 1 tsp. garlic; minced.
- 1 tsp. parsley
- 1 tsp. paprika
- 1 tbsp. olive oil
- Salt and pepper to taste

Directions:

1. Mix breadcrumbs, salt, pepper, paprika and oil. Mix well to make a thick paste. Mix chopped chicken, ketchup, one egg, parsley in a bowl
2. Shape the chicken mixture into little nugget shapes and dip into other beaten egg. Coat the nuggets with breadcrumbs. Cook at 390 °F for 10 minutes in air fryer.

Lamb and Macadamia Nuts Mix

Preparation time: 10 minutes

Cooking time: 20 minutes

Servings: 4

Ingredients:

- 1 cup baby spinach
- 2 pounds lamb stew meat, cubed
- 2 tablespoons macadamia nuts, peeled
- ½ cup beef stock
- 2 garlic cloves, minced
- Salt and black pepper to the taste
- 1 tablespoon oregano, chopped

Directions:

1. In the air fryer's pan, mix the lamb with the nuts and the other ingredients,
2. cook at 380 degrees F for 20 minutes,
3. divide between plates and serve.

Nutrition:

Calories 280, Fat 12, Fiber 8, Carbs 20, Protein 19

Beef, Cucumber and Eggplants

Preparation time: 10 minutes

Cooking time: 20 minutes

Servings: 4

Ingredients:

- 1 pound beef stew meat, cut into strips
- 2 cucumbers, sliced
- 2 eggplants, cubed
- 2 garlic cloves, minced
- 1 cup heavy cream
- 2 tablespoons olive oil
- Salt and black pepper to the taste

Directions:

1. In a baking dish that fits your air fryer, mix the beef with the eggplants and the other ingredients, toss, introduce the pan in the fryer and cook at 400 degrees F for 20 minutes.
2. Divide everything into bowls and serve.

Nutrition:

Calories 283, Fat 11, Fiber 9, Carbs 22, Protein 14

Spicy Lamb Kebabs

Preparation Time: 20 minutes

Cooking Time: 8 minutes

Servings: 6

Ingredients:

- 4 eggs, beaten

- 1 pound ground lamb
- 1 cup pistachios, chopped
- 4 tablespoons plain flour
- 4 tablespoons flat-leaf parsley, chopped
- 4 garlic cloves, minced
- Olive oil
- 2 teaspoons chili flakes
- 2 tablespoons fresh lemon juice
- 2 teaspoons cumin seeds
- 1 teaspoon fennel seeds
- 2 teaspoons dried mint
- 2 teaspoons salt
- 1 teaspoon coriander seeds
- 1 teaspoon freshly ground black pepper

Directions:

1. Preheat the Air fryer to 355 degrees F and grease an Air fryer basket.
2. Mix lamb, pistachios, eggs, lemon juice, chili flakes, flour, cumin seeds, fennel seeds, coriander seeds, mint, parsley, salt and black pepper in a large bowl.

3. Thread the lamb mixture onto metal skewers to form sausages and coat with olive oil.
4. Place the skewers in the Air fryer basket and cook for about 8 minutes.
5. Dish out in a platter and serve hot.

Nutrition:

Calories: 284, Fat: 15.8g, Carbohydrates: 8.4g, Sugar: 1.1g, Protein: 27.9g, Sodium: 932mg

Pepper Pork Chops

Preparation Time: 15 minutes

Cooking Time: 6 minutes

Servings: 2

Ingredients:

- 2 pork chops
- 1 egg white
- ¾ cup xanthum gum
- ¼ teaspoon freshly ground black pepper
- ½ teaspoon sea salt
- 1 oil mister

Directions:

1. Preheat the Air fryer to 400 degrees F and grease an Air fryer basket.
2. Whisk egg white with salt and black pepper in a bowl and dip the pork chops in it.
3. Cover the bowl and marinate for about 20 minutes.

4. Pour the xanthum gum over both sides of the chops and spray with oil mister.
5. Arrange the chops in the Air fryer basket and cook for about 6 minutes.
6. Dish out in a bowl and serve warm.

Nutrition:

Calories: 541, Fat: 34g, Carbohydrates: 3.4g, Sugar: 1g, Protein: 20.3g, Sodium: 547mg

Pork Chops with Chicory Treviso

Preparation time: 10-20;

Cooking time: 0-15;

Serve: 2

Ingredients:

- 4 pork chops
- 40g butter
- 1 chicory stalk
- Flour to taste
- Salt to taste

Directions:

1. Cut the chicory into small pieces. Place the butter and chicory in pieces on the air fryer's basket previously preheated at 180 °C and brown for 2 min.
2. Add the previously floured and salted pork slices (directly over the chicory), simmer for 6 minutes turning them over after 3 minutes.

3. Remove the slices and place them on a serving plate, covering them with the rest of the red chicory juice collected at the bottom of the basket.

Nutrition:

Calories 504, Fat 33, Carbohydrates 0g, Sugars 0g, Protein 42g, Cholesterol 130mg

Beef and Celery

Preparation Time: 65 minutes

Servings: 6

Ingredients:

- 1 lb. yellow onion; chopped.
- 3 cups beef stock
- 1 lb. celery; chopped.
- 16 oz. canned tomatoes; chopped.
- 3 lbs. beef roast
- 2 tbsp. olive oil
- Salt and black pepper to taste

Directions:

1. Place all the ingredients into a baking dish that fits your air fryer and mix well
2. Put the pan in the fryer and cook at 390 °F for 55 minutes
3. Slice the roast and then divide it and the celery mix between plates. Serve and enjoy!

Beef Kabobs Recipe

Preparation Time: 20 Minutes

Servings: 4

Ingredients:

- 2 red bell peppers; chopped
- 2-pound sirloin steak; cut into medium pieces
- 1 red onion; chopped
- 2 tbsp. chili powder
- 2 tbsp. hot sauce
- Juice form 1 lime
- 1 zucchini; sliced
- 1/2 tbsp. cumin; ground
- 1/4 cup olive oil
- 1/4 cup salsa
- Salt and black pepper to the taste

Directions:

1. In a bowl; mix salsa with lime juice, oil, hot sauce, chili powder, cumin, salt and black pepper and whisk well.

2. Divide meat bell peppers, zucchini and onion on skewers, brush kabobs with the salsa mix you made earlier, put them in your preheated air fryer and cook them for 10 minutes at 370 °F, flipping kabobs halfway. Divide among plates and serve with a side salad

Sautéed Green Beans

Preparation Time: 20 minutes

Servings: 2

Ingredients:

- 8-oz fresh green beans, trimmed and cut in half
- 1 tsp. sesame oil
- 1 tbsp. soy sauce

Directions:

1. In a bowl; mix well green beans, soy sauce and sesame oil.
2. Set the temperature of air fryer to 390 °F. Lightly, grease an air fryer basket.
3. Arrange green beans into the prepared air fryer basket. Air fry for about 10 minutes, tossing once halfway through.
4. Remove from air fryer and transfer the green beans onto serving plates. Serve hot.

Simple Kale Chicken Soup

Preparation Time: 5 minutes

Cooking Time: 15 minutes

Servings: 4

Ingredients:

- 2 cups chicken breast, cooked and chopped
- 2 tsp. garlic, minced
- 4 cups vegetable broth

- ½ tsp. cinnamon
- 1 onion, diced
- 12 oz. kale
- 1 tsp. salt

Directions:

1. Add all ingredients into air fryer and stir well.
2. Secure pot with lid and cook on manual high pressure for 5 minutes.
3. Allow pressure to release naturally for 10 minutes, then release using quick release Directions.
4. Stir well and serve warm.

Nutrition:

Calories – 158 Protein – 19.7 g.Fat – 2.8 g. Carbs – 13.1 g.

Healthy Chicken Vegetable Soup

Preparation Time: 5 minutes

Cooking Time: 14 minutes

Servings: 6

Ingredients:

- 2 chicken breasts, cut into cubes
- ½ tsp. red pepper flakes
- 1 tsp. garlic powder
- ¼ cup fresh parsley, chopped
- 3 cups chicken broth
- 14 oz. can tomatoes, diced
- ¼ cup cabbage, shredded
- ½ cup frozen corn
- 1 cup frozen green beans
- ¼ cup frozen peas
- 2 celery stalks, chopped
- 1 carrot, peeled and cubed
- ½ sweet potato, peeled and cubed
- 3 garlic cloves, minced

- ½ onion, chopped
- 1 tsp. salt
- ½ tsp. pepper

Directions:

1. Add all ingredients into air fryer and stir well.
2. Secure pot with lid and cook on manual high pressure for 4 minutes.
3. Allow pressure to release naturally for 10 minutes, then release using quick release Directions.
4. Stir well and serve.

Nutrition:

Calories – 171 Protein – 18.9 g. Fat – 4.6 g. Carbs – 13.9 g.

Chicken Rice Noodle Soup

Preparation Time: 5 minutes

Cooking Time: 10 minutes

Servings: 6

Ingredients:

- 1 bell pepper, chopped
- 6 cups chicken, cooked and cubed
- 2 ½ cups cabbage, shredded
- 2 tbsp. fresh ginger, grated
- 3 tbsp. rice vinegar
- 2 tbsp. soy sauce
- 3 garlic cloves, minced
- 8 oz. rice noodles
- 1 large carrot, peeled and sliced
- 6 cups chicken stock
- 2 celery stalks, sliced
- 1 onion, chopped
- ½ tsp. black pepper

Directions:

1. Add all ingredients into air fryer and stir well.
2. Secure pot with lid and cook on manual high pressure for 10 minutes.
3. Quick release pressure then open the lid.
4. Stir well and serve.

Nutrition:

Calories – 306 Protein – 43.1 g. Fat – 5.1 g. Carbs – 18.7 g.

Asparagus Garlic Ham Soup

Preparation Time: 15 minutes

Cooking Time: 50 minutes

Servings: 4

Ingredients:

- 1 ½ lbs. asparagus, chopped
- 2 tsp. garlic, minced
- 4 cups chicken stock
- 3 tbsp. olive oil
- 1 onion, diced
- ¾ cup ham, diced
- ½ tsp. thyme

Directions:

1. Add oil into air fryer and set on Sauté mode.
2. Add onion and sauté for 4 minutes.
3. Add garlic and ham and cook for a minute.
4. Add stock and thyme. Stir well.

5. Seal pot with lid and cook on Soup mode for 45 minutes.
6. Quick release pressure then open the lid,
7. Stir well and serve.

Nutrition:

Calories – 188 Protein – 9 g. Fat – 13.5 g. Carbs – 11.4 g.

Air fryer Greek Beef Stew

Preparation Time: 15 minutes

Cooking Time: 40 minutes

Servings: 4

Ingredients:

- 1 ½ pounds stew beef cut into small cubes
- 8 small potatoes
- 8 small onions
- ¼ cup of butter
- 2-3 carrots, sliced
- ¾ cups tomato paste
- 1 teaspoon cinnamon

Directions:

1. Set air fryer to saute mode and cook beef in the butter until browned. This will take about 5 minutes. Then remove.
2. Put in the onions to the pot and saute about 5 minutes.

3. Stop saute mode. Add beef back to the pot and then add carrots, potatoes, tomato paste, and cinnamon. Add 2-3 cups of water.
4. Lock the lid and set pressure to high and cook for 35 minutes.
5. Allow steam to release naturally for 10 minutes and then quick release remaining pressure.
6. Ready to serve.

Nutrition:

Calories – 479 Protein – 43 g. Fat – 20 g. Carbs – 31 g.

Mushroom Chicken Soup

Preparation Time: 10 minutes

Cooking Time: 25 minutes

Servings: 4

Ingredients:

- 1 lb. chicken breast, cut into chunks
- 1 tsp. Italian seasoning
- 1 small yellow squash, chopped
- 2 ½ cups chicken stock
- 2 cups mushrooms, sliced
- 2 garlic cloves, minced
- 1 onion, sliced
- 1 tsp. black pepper
- 1 tsp. salt

Directions:

1. Add all ingredients into air fryer and stir well.
2. Secure pot with lid and cook on manual high pressure for 15 minutes.

3. Allow pressure to release naturally for 10 minutes, then release using quick release Directions.
4. Remove chicken from pot and puree the vegetable mixture using a blender.
5. Shred the chicken using a fork. Return shredded chicken to the pot and stir well.
6. Serve and enjoy.

Nutrition:

Calories – 166 Protein – 26.4 g. Fat – 3.8 g. Carbs – 6.1 g.

Classic ratatouille (Vegan)

Preparation time: 30 minutes

Servings: 2

Ingredients

- 1 tbsp olive oil
- 2 garlic cloves, minced
- 3 roma tomatoes, thinly sliced

- 1 zucchini, thinly sliced
- 2 yellow bell peppers, sliced
- 1 tbsp vinegar
- 2 tbsp herbs de provence
- Salt and black pepper to taste

Directions

1. Preheat air fryer on air fry function to 390 degrees F and place all ingredients in a bowl.
2. Season with salt and pepper and stir until the veggies are well coated.
3. Arrange the vegetable in a round baking dish and place in the oven.
4. Cook for 15 minutes, shaking occasionally.
5. Let sit for 5 more minutes after the timer goes off.

Nutrition:

Calories: 261, Protein: 5.7g, Fat: 14.54g, Carbs: 32.04g

Curried Eggplant (Vegan)

Servings: 2

Preparation Time: 15 minutes

Cooking Time: 10 minutes

Ingredients

- 1 large eggplant, cut into ½-inch thick slices
- ½ fresh red chili, chopped
- 1 garlic clove, minced
- 1 tablespoon vegetable oil
- ¼ teaspoon curry powder
- Salt, as required

Directions:

1. Set the temperature of air fryer to 300 degrees F. Grease an air fryer basket.
2. In a bowl, add all the ingredients and toss to coat well.
3. Arrange eggplant slices into the prepared air fryer basket in a single layer.

4. Air fry for about 10 minutes, shaking once halfway through.
5. Remove from air fryer and transfer the eggplant slices onto serving plates.
6. Serve hot.

Nutrition:

Calories: 121, Carbohydrate: 14.2g, Protein: 2.4g, Fat: 7.3g, Sugar: 7g, Sodium: 83mg

Stuffed Tomatoes (Vegan)

Servings: 4

Preparation Time: 15 minutes

Cooking Time: 22 minutes

Ingredients

- 4 tomatoes
- 1 cup frozen peas, thawed
- 1 carrot, peeled and finely chopped
- 1 teaspoon olive oil
- 1 onion, chopped
- 1 garlic clove, minced
- 2 cups cold cooked rice
- 1 tablespoon soy sauce

Directions:

1. Cut the top of each tomato and scoop out pulp and seeds.
2. In a skillet, heat oil over low heat and sauté the carrot, onion, garlic, and peas for about 2 minutes.

3. Stir in the soy sauce and rice and remove from heat.
4. Set the temperature of air fryer to 355 degrees F. Grease an air fryer basket.
5. Stuff each tomato with the rice mixture.
6. Arrange tomatoes into the prepared air fryer basket.
7. Air fry for about 20 minutes.
8. Remove from air fryer and transfer the tomatoes onto a serving platter.
9. Set aside to cool slightly.
10. Serve warm.

Nutrition:

Calories: 421, Carbohydrate: 89.1g, Protein: 10.5g, Fat: 2.2g, Sugar: 7.2g, Sodium: 277mg

Sweet and Spicy Grilled Chicken

Servings: 4

Cooking Time: 35 minutes

Ingredients:

- ½ cup brown sugar
- 2 tablespoons chili powder
- ½ teaspoon garlic powder
- 1 teaspoon liquid smoke seasoning

- 1 teaspoon salt
- 4 boneless chicken breasts

Directions

1. Place all ingredients in a Ziploc bag and give a good shake. Allow marinating in the fridge for at least 2 hours.
2. Preheat the air fryer at 375 degree F.
3. Place the grill pan accessory in the air fryer.
4. Grill the chicken for 35 minutes.
5. Make sure to flip the chicken every 10 minutes to grill evenly.

Nutrition

Calories: 446; Carbs: 29.6g; Protein: 61.8g; Fat: 7.7g

Honey Lime Grilled Chicken

Servings: 4

Cooking Time: 40 minutes

Ingredients:

- 2 pounds boneless chicken breasts
- ½ cup honey
- 2 tablespoons soy sauce
- ¼ cup lime juice, freshly squeezed

- 1 tablespoon olive oil
- 2 cloves of garlic, minced
- ½ cup cilantro, chopped finely
- Salt and pepper to taste

Directions

1. Place all ingredients in a Ziploc bag and give a good shake. Allow marinating in the fridge for at least 2 hours.
2. Preheat the air fryer at 375 degrees F.
3. Place the grill pan accessory in the air fryer.
4. Grill the chicken for 40 minutes making sure to flip the chicken every 10 minutes to grill evenly on all sides.

Nutrition

Calories:467; Carbs: 38.9g; Protein:52.5 g; Fat: 10.2g

Pesto Grilled Chicken

Servings: 8

Cooking Time: 30 minutes

Ingredients:

- 8 chicken thighs
- 1 ¾ cup of your favorite pesto
- Salt and pepper to taste

Directions

1. Place all ingredients in the Ziploc bag and allow to marinate in the fridge for at least 2 hours.
2. Preheat the air fryer at 375 degrees F.
3. Place the grill pan accessory in the air fryer.
4. Grill the chicken for at least 30 minutes.
5. Make sure to flip the chicken every 10 minutes for even grilling.

Nutrition

Calories: 481; Carbs: 3.8g; Protein: 32.6g; Fat: 36.8g

Easy Curry Grilled Chicken Wings

Servings: 4

Cooking Time: 35 minutes

Ingredients:

- 2 pounds chicken wings
- 1 tablespoons curry powder
- ½ cup plain yogurt
- Salt and pepper to taste

Directions

1. Season the chicken wings with yogurt, curry powder, salt, and pepper. Toss to combine everything.
2. Allow marinating in the fridge for at least 2 hours.
3. Preheat the air fryer at 375 degrees F.
4. Place the grill pan accessory in the air fryer.
5. Grill the chicken for 35 minutes and make sure to flip the chicken halfway through the cooking time.

Nutrition

Calories:314; Carbs: 3.3g; Protein: 51.3g; Fat: 9.2g

PiriPiri Chicken

Servings: 6

Cooking Time: 45 minutes

Ingredients:

- 3 pounds chicken breasts
- ½ cup piripiri sauce
- ¼ cup fresh lemon juice
- 1-inch fresh ginger, peeled, and sliced thinly
- 1 large shallot, quartered
- Salt and pepper to taste
- 3 cloves of garlic, minced

Directions

1. Preheat the air fryer at 375 degrees F.
2. Place the grill pan accessory in the air fryer.
3. On a large piece of foil, place the chicken and top with the rest of the ingredients.
4. Fold the foil and crimp the edges.
5. Grill for 45 minutes.

Nutrition

Calories:404; Carbs: 3.4g; Protein: 47.9g; Fat: 21.1g

Air Fryer Plantains

Preparation Time: 10 minutes

Cooking Time: 10 minutes

Servings: 4

Ingredients:

- 2 ripe plantains
- 2 teaspoons avocado oil

- 1/8 teaspoon salt

Directions:

1. Preheat the Air fryer to 400 degrees F and grease an Air fryer basket.
2. Mix the plantains with avocado oil and salt in a bowl.
3. Arrange the coated plantains in the Air fryer basket and cook for about 10 minutes.
4. Dish out in a bowl and serve immediately.

Nutrition:

Calories: 112, Fat: 0.6g, Carbohydrates: 28.7g, Sugar: 13.4g, Protein: 1.2g, Sodium: 77mg

Healthy Veggie Lasagna

Preparation Time: 15 minutes

Cooking Time: 1 hour; Serves 4

Ingredients:

- 1½ pounds pumpkin, peeled and chopped finely
- ¾ pound tomatoes, cubed
- ½ pound fresh lasagna sheets
- 1 pound cooked beets, sliced thinly
- ¼ cup Parmesan cheese, grated
- 2 tablespoons sunflower oil

Directions:

1. Preheat the Air fryer to 300 degrees F and lightly grease a baking dish.
2. Put pumpkin and 1 tablespoon sunflower oil in a skillet and cook for about 10 minutes.
3. Put the pumpkin mixture and tomatoes in a blender and pulse until smooth.

4. Return to the skillet and cook on low heat for about 5 minutes.
5. Transfer the pumpkin puree into the baking dish and layer with lasagna sheets.
6. Top with the beet slices and cheese and place in the Air fryer.
7. Cook for about 45 minutes and dish out to serve warm.

Nutrition:

Calories: 368, Fats: 10.3g, Carbohydrates: 59.8g, Sugar: 16.9g, Proteins: 13.4g, Sodium: 165mg

Dark Chocolate Cheesecake

Preparation Time: 20 minutes

Cooking Time: 34 minutes

Servings: 6

Ingredients:

- 1 cup dark chocolate, chopped
- 3 eggs, whites and yolks separated
- ½ cup cream cheese, softened

- 2 tablespoons cocoa powder
- ¼ cup dates jam
- 2 tablespoons powdered sugar

Directions:
1. Preheat the Air fryer to 285 °F and grease a cake pan lightly.
2. Refrigerate egg whites in a bowl to chill before using.
3. Microwave chocolate and cream cheese on high for about 3 minutes.
4. Remove from microwave and whisk in the egg yolks.
5. Whisk together egg whites until firm peaks form and combine with the chocolate mixture.
6. Transfer the mixture into a cake pan and arrange in the Air fryer basket.
7. Cook for about 30 minutes and dish out.
8. Dust with powdered sugar and spread dates jam on top to serve.

Nutrition:

Calories: 298, Fat: 18.3g, Carbohydrates: 29.7g, Sugar: 24.5g, Protein: 6.3g, Sodium: 119mg

Lemon Coconut Pie

Preparation Time: 10 minutes

Cooking time: 35 minutes

Servings: 8

Ingredients:

- 2 eggs, whisked
- ¾ cup swerve

- ¼ cup coconut flour
- ½ teaspoon lemon extract
- 1 teaspoon lemon zest, grated
- 2 tablespoons butter, melted
- 1 teaspoon baking powder
- 1 teaspoon vanilla extract
- 4 ounces coconut, shredded
- Cooking spray

Directions:

1. In a bowl, combine all the Ingredients: except the cooking spray and stir well.
2. Grease a pie pan that fits the air fryer with the cooking spray, pour the mixture inside, put the pan in the air fryer and cook at 360 degrees F for 35 minutes.
3. Slice and serve warm.

Nutrition:

Calories 212, fat 15, fiber 2, carbs 6, protein 4

Pumpkin Cake

Preparation Time: 35 minutes

Servings: 8

Ingredients:

- 1 egg; whisked
- 8 oz. canned pumpkin puree
- 1/2 cup Greek yogurt

- 3/4 tsp. pumpkin pie spice
- 3/4 cup sugar
- 1 tsp. baking powder
- 1 cup white flour
- Cooking spray

Directions:

1. Place all ingredients: other than the cooking spraying a bowl and mix well.
2. Grease a cake pan with cooking spray, pour the cake batter inside and spread
3. Place the pan in the air fryer and cook at 330°F for 25 minutes. Let the cake cool down, slice and serve.

Easy Baked Chocolate Mug Cake

Servings: 3

Cooking Time: 15 minutes

Ingredients

- ½ cup cocoa powder
- ½ cup stevia powder
- 1 package cream cheese, room temperature

- 1 cup coconut cream
- 1 tablespoon vanilla extract
- 4 tablespoons butter

Directions:

1. Preheat the air fryer for 5 minutes.
2. In a mixing bowl, combine all ingredients.
3. Use a hand mixer to mix everything until fluffy.
4. Pour into greased mugs.
5. Place the mugs in the fryer basket.
6. Bake for 15 minutes at 350 degrees F.
7. Place in the fridge to chill before serving.

Nutrition:

Calories: 744; Carbohydrates: 15.3 g; Protein: 13.9g; Fat: 69.7g

Crisped 'n Chewy Chonut Holes

Servings: 6

Cooking Time: 10 minutes

Ingredients

- ¼ cup almond milk
- ¼ cup coconut sugar
- 1 cup white all-purpose flour
- ¼ teaspoon cinnamon
- ½ teaspoon salt
- 1 tablespoon coconut oil, melted
- 1 teaspoon baking powder
- 2 tablespoon aquafaba or liquid from canned chickpeas

Directions:

1. In a mixing bowl, mix the flour, sugar, and baking powder. Add the salt and cinnamon and mix well.

2. In another bowl, mix together the coconut oil, aquafaba, and almond milk.
3. Gently pour the dry ingredients to the wet ingredients. Mix together until well combined or until you form a sticky dough.
4. Place the dough in the refrigerator to rest for at least an hour.
5. Preheat the air fryer to 370 °F.
6. Create small balls of the dough and place inside the air fryer, and cook for 10 minutes. Do not shake the air fryer.
7. Once cooked, sprinkle with sugar and cinnamon.
8. Serve with your breakfast coffee.

Nutrition:

Calories: 120; Carbohydrates: 21.62g; Protein: 2.31g; Fat:2.76g

Cream Puffs

Preparation Time: 21 minutes

Servings: 8 puffs

Ingredients:

- 1 large egg.
- 2 oz. full-fat cream cheese.
- ¼ cup powdered erythritol
- ½ cup blanched finely ground almond flour.

- ½ cup low-carb vanilla protein powder
- ½ cup granular erythritol.
- 2 tbsp. heavy whipping cream.
- 5 tbsp. unsalted butter; melted.
- ½ tsp. baking powder.
- ¼ tsp. ground cinnamon.
- ½ tsp. vanilla extract.

Directions:

1. Mix almond flour, protein powder, granular erythritol, baking powder, egg and butter in a large bowl until a soft dough forms.
2. Place the dough in the freezer for 20 minutes. Wet your hands with water and roll the dough into eight balls.
3. Cut a piece of parchment to fit your air fryer basket. Working in batches as necessary, place the dough balls into the air fryer basket on top of parchment.
4. Adjust the temperature to 380 Degrees F and set the timer for 6 minutes. Flip cream puffs halfway through the cooking time.

5. When the timer beeps, remove the puffs and allow to cool.
6. Take a medium bowl, beat the cream cheese, powdered erythritol, cinnamon, cream and vanilla until fluffy.
7. Place the mixture into a pastry bag or a storage bag with the end snipped. Cut a small hole in the bottom of each puff and fill with some of the cream mixture. Store in an airtight container up to 2 days in the refrigerator.

Nutrition:

Calories: 178; Protein: 14.9g; Fiber: 1.3g; Fat: 12.1g; Carbs: 22.1g

Notes

www.ingramcontent.com/pod-product-compliance
Lightning Source LLC
Chambersburg PA
CBHW070933080526
44589CB00013B/1502